The Ladies Flower Garden

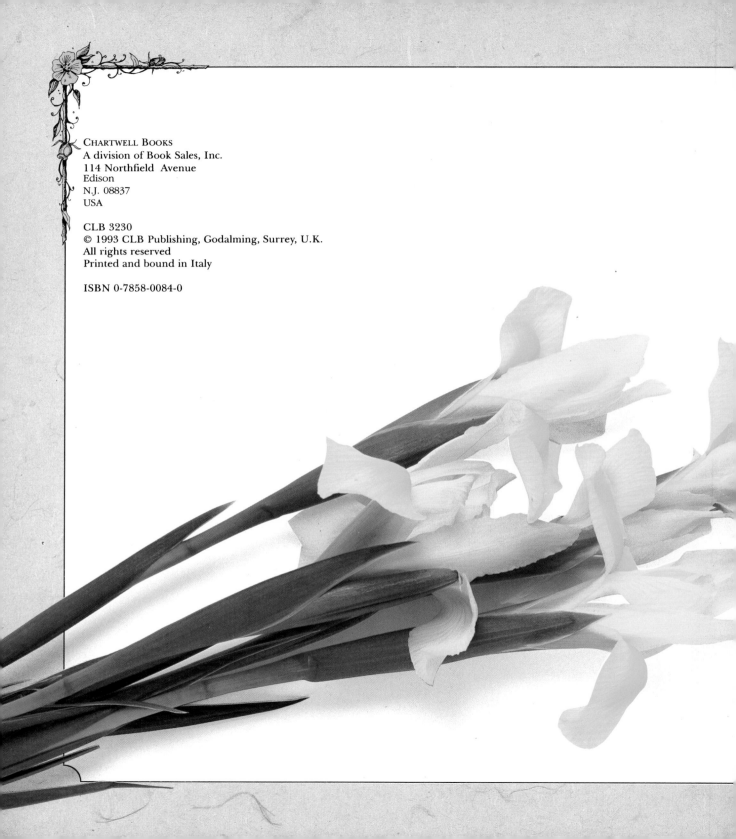

CHARTWELL BOOKS
A division of Book Sales, Inc.
114 Northfield Avenue
Edison
N.J. 08837
USA

CLB 3230
© 1993 CLB Publishing, Godalming, Surrey, U.K.
All rights reserved
Printed and bound in Italy

ISBN 0-7858-0084-0

The Ladies' Flower Garden

Compiled and written by Wendy Hobson

CHARTWELL
BOOKS, INC.

The Beauty of Flowers

The exquisite beauty of a perfect rose, the delicate fragrance of freesias, the flaming colour of a bank of tulips – what could be more wonderful than to fill your garden and your home with flowers? Throughout history, flowers have been an important part of life not only for their beauty, but also for their colour, their fragrance, and for the almost magical way they can express or transform our mood. Who does not feel a lift when confronted with an exuberant display of bright summer flowers? What is more touching than to receive a tiny posy of woodland blooms as a child's gift? Is there anything more romantic than a single fragrant red rose tied with silken ribbon?

Those who already love flowers will need no persuading that a succession of varied and fascinating blooms give life, colour and meaning to any garden. Those awakening to the potential to be found among garden flowers need only take a stroll past some well tended gardens to see what a difference is made even by a few simple flowers.

The vast range of species and varieties to choose from need not be daunting, for there are many flowers which are a simple pleasure to grow. Just by looking in your garden, you will be able to tell whether it is sunny or shady and whether your soil is wet clay or dry sand, which will help you in your choices. Look around at other gardens close to your home and see which flowers thrive there. Old favourites - lupins, nasturtium, roses, phlox – are often a good choice. In the past, gardeners had a lot less leisure time to tend their gardens than we do now, so the flowers that became popular were those which gave a beautiful display with the minimum of cost and effort. Gardening books, magazines or nursery and garden centre staff can also be of immense help in your planning and selection.

However beautifully decorated, a house without flowers does not have the welcoming, vibrant feel which a vase of colourful flowers can bring. Huge displays of expensive flowers need only be for special occasions. A few blooms from the garden or a bunch of seasonal flowers from the florist cost so little in terms of money and effort but make so much difference to the aspect of a room.

Those who love to arrange flowers often like to extend their creative skills into other crafts: preparing dried flowers for winter arrangements or gifts, using silk or paper flowers, pressing the most perfect petals to preserve their beauty.

The Ladies' Flower Garden offers you a source of ideas, inspiration, practical tips and guidelines to help you make yours a world of flowers.

The Language of Flowers

We all associate the red rose with love and the white lily with purity, but sadly few other flower associations are common knowledge today.

It was not always so, however. Historically, flowers were used almost as much for their symbolic meaning as for their beauty, and carefully selected blooms or bouquets were often used to convey very specific intentions. In Victorian times in particular – when the code of etiquette was extremely strict, particularly between a young man and the object of his affections – a gift of a posy could secretly tell the recipient almost as much as a letter – providing, of course, they had read the same books, for flower books often disagreed on the meanings attributed to each flower. How the gift was received could also speak volumes. A flower touched to the lips meant 'yes', but a plucked petal fluttering to the ground meant disappointment to any eager suitor.

Flowers make wonderful gifts for any occasion, so why not think about the meaning of the flowers you are giving and create a posy or a bouquet which expresses the feeling behind the gift. The gift tag can explain the meanings of the flowers, if you wish, or perhaps you would like to indulge in a little intrigue and let the recipient discover the meanings for themselves.

Almond	*hope*
Alyssum	*worth beyond beauty*
Amaranth	*hopelessness*
Amaryllis	*splendid beauty*
Anemone	*forsaken*
Antirrhinum	*refusal*
Apple blossom	*temptation*
Bluebell	*constancy*
Canterbury bell	*constancy*
Camellia	*excellence*
Campanula	*gratitude*
Carnation, red	*heart-forsaken*
Carnation, striped	*refusal*
Carnation, white	*disdain*
Christmas rose	*scandal*
Chrysanthemum, red	*I love you*
Chrysanthemum, white	*truth*
Chrysanthemum, yellow	*slighted love*
Clematis	*mental beauty*
Convolvulus	*fleeting joy*
Crocus	*youthful gladness*
Cyclamen	*diffidence*
Daffodil	*regard*
Dahlia	*pomp*

Daisy	*innocence*
Elderflower	*compassion*
Fennel	*flattery*
Forget-me-not	*true love*
Foxglove	*insincerity*
Fuchsia	*gracefulness*
Geranium, red	*comfort*
Heather	*solitude*
Honesty	*honesty*
Honeysuckle	*generous affection*
Hyacinth, purple	*sorrow*
Hyacinth, blue	*constancy*

Ivy	*friendship*
Jasmine	*amiability*
Larkspur	*infidelity*
Lavender	*distrust*
Lilac	*first love*
Lily, water	*purity of heart*
Lily, white	*purity*
Lily, yellow	*falsehood*
Lily-of-the-valley	*return of happiness*
Magnolia	*love of nature*
Marigold	*grief*
Marigold, French	*jealousy*
Mesembryanthemum	*idleness*
Mint	*wisdom*
Myrtle	*love*
Narcissus	*self-interest*
Nasturtium	*patriotism*
Pansy	*thoughts*
Poppy, red	*consolation*
Poppy, white	*sleep*
Ranunculus	*you are dazzling*
Rhododendron	*danger*

Rose, red	*love*
Rose, white	*I am worthy of you*
Rose, yellow	*jealousy*
Rosebud	*young love*
Rosemary	*remembrance*
Rue	*disdain*
Salvia	*energy*
Snowdrop	*consolation and hope*
Sunflower	*haughtiness*
Sweet pea	*departure*
Tulip	*fame*
Tulip, red	*declaration of love*
Tulip, yellow	*hopeless love*
Violet	*modesty*
Wallflower	*affection*
Yew	*sadness*

Arranging Flowers

Arranging flowers can be as simple as placing a bright bunch of daffodils in a plain vase, or you can spend time designing and creating a fabulous arrangement. Whatever you do, a few tips on how to go about it can be useful before you start.

Equipment

For the simplest displays of flowers, all you need are a pair of sharp scissors and a jam jar, but you will find that a few extra items of florists' equipment will make it easier for you to create the effects you envisage when you start your arrangement. They are all available from florists or hardware stores and none is expensive.

Sharp scissors and a sharp knife are important for cutting stems neatly. Secateurs can be useful for woody stems, and a long-bladed knife for cutting dry foam.

To hold flowers in position, the simplest thing to use is dry foam. This can be wedged into a vase, or held firm in a container by placing it on a plastic or metal florists' spike kept in place with adhesive clay which you can buy in a long strip. For incurving bowls, chicken wire can be cut and pressed into the container to hold the stems in place. If necessary, you can cover foam or wire with a little moss. Glass marbles look attractive in glass containers and also hold stems in place.

If you need to wire stems for a tall arrangement, you can buy various thickness of stub wires suitable for different kinds of flowers. The wires are bound to the stem with thick or thin reel wire and then covered with gutta-percha tape, ribbon or raffia. Plastic funnels are also available which you can press into foam to help create taller arrangements.

Containers

The only limit to the type of containers you can use for your flower arrangements is that they must be waterproof. For the best effects, select containers which suit the style, colour and size of the flowers so that the container becomes part of the overall effect. Tiny flowers, for example, will be dwarfed by an oversized vase, while delicate flowers will not look their best in a chunky terracotta pot. Use a variety of containers, from ceramic vases in any shape, colour or size, to glass vases, terracotta or metal containers or baskets lined with a plastic bowl. Don't forget unusual containers, especially for small arrangements: large shells, boxes, silver vases and so on. Let your imagination lead you.

If you have nothing you think will be suitable, improvise. Repaint an old vase or add stencils to a plain one. Wrap a piece of attractive fabric round a vase and secure it at the top with a stitch or a pin. Line the inside of a glass vase with a mosaic of coloured or silvered papers and varnish it for a wonderfully different effect.

Preparing the flowers

If you cut flowers from the garden, choose the coolest part of the day and try to avoid cutting them in full sun. Select flowers which are in full bud so that you can enjoy watching the buds open and so that the arrangement lasts as long as possible.

Whether cut from the garden or purchased from the florist, flowers need a long drink before you start to arrange them. Holding the stems underwater, use a sharp knife or scissors to cut the stems diagonally to expose the maximum surface area to the water. Strip the leaves and any side shoots from the bottom of the stems which will be in the vase.

If you then take the time to prepare the stems, the flowers will last longer. Treat soft stems gently to avoid bruising them. Sear the end of sappy stems with a flame. Once cut, fill hollow stems with water and plug them with cotton wool. Strip a little bark from woody stems and crush the base or split it with a knife. Wrap tulip stems or flowers with bendy stems closely with newspaper to prevent them twisting.

Once prepared, stand the flowers in a bucket of tepid water in a cool place for at least a few hours.

Wiring flowers

Wiring stems helps to keep them straight and in position in your arrangement. Stub wires of an appropriate thickness can simply be inserted into hollow stems. Otherwise, bind the wire to the stem using reel wire. To cover the wire, hold the flower head downwards and place the end of a piece of gutta-percha tape diagonally against the top of the stem. Holding the tape taut, twist the stem so that the tape spirals up the wire.

Caring for your arrangements

Select a suitable position for your flowers out of direct heat or sunlight and where they will not be disturbed. Add a few drops of bleach and a teaspoon of sugar to the water in the vase before arranging your flowers and replace the water regularly to keep it fresh. Remove any dead flowers from the arrangement to keep it looking lovely for as long as possible.

Making a bouquet

Prepare and wrap a bouquet only a short time before you present it so that the flowers do not wilt. Start with the tallest flowers, laying them down on a table in the shape you want, then gradually build up with smaller and smaller flowers. Choose a paper which complements the arrangement, or wrap in cellophane so that you can see the lovely flowers. Place the bouquet at an angle across the top of the paper. Lift the lower corner over the flowers then bring the far corner over and round the flowers and secure with tape. Fold the corner over the top of the bouquet and secure with tape. Decorate the stem end with ribbon bows with curled flowing ribbons.

Preserving Flowers

W e do not always have the time to prepare fresh flower arrangements, and in the winter materials may be scarce or expensive, so it can be wonderful to preserve the beauty of flowers to use in dried arrangements to enjoy all the year round.

A vast range of dried flower materials are now available in florists and craft shops, but it is very satisfying if you can preserve some of your own flowers.

Suitable materials

The most popular of all the dried flowers are helichrysum, or straw flowers, as they are available in almost every colour and have the perfect texture for drying. Other suitable flowers include amaranth, astilbe, tiny dahlias, delphinium, cornflowers, golden rod, larkspur, mimosa, roses, statice, sunray and yarrow.

Many different grasses and reeds are perfect for dried arrangements, providing wonderful tall, feathery stems in ranges of gold, yellow and pink, and leaves such as copper beech or eucalyptus are also attractive. Chinese lanterns, seeded sorrel, nigella, clematis or poppy seed heads and the beautiful silver seed cases of honesty provide range and variety.

Herbs are obvious choices for drying: sage, dill, rosemary and a range of other herbs impart subtle fragrance as well as beauty to a dried arrangement.

Containers and equipment

Everything which you can use for a fresh flower arrangement is suitable for making dried arrangements except, of course, that you do not need the containers to be waterproof. This is where baskets

come into their own, as their rustic charm and subtle colouring lend themselves perfectly to delicate dried blooms.

Air drying

This is the simplest method of drying plant materials and all you need is a cool, well-ventilated room such as a spare room, loft or cool airing cupboard. It is essential that the air can circulate round the flowers and leaves, otherwise they may rot before drying out.

Small flowers can be hung upside down to dry in small bunches of about five blooms. Make sure the stems are sound and the flowers are approaching full bloom. If you think the stems may break while drying, wire them before hanging (see page x). Once the flowers are dry, it may be necessary to wire the stems if they are brittle. Cut off the lower leaves and any damaged leaves or thorns and tie the base of the stems with string or raffia so that

Preserving in glycerine

This method is used mainly for leaves and will maintain the flexibility of the plant material. Cut the stems at an angle as you would for a fresh arrangement and remove the lower leaves. Stand the stems in water for a few hours. Make a solution of 40 per cent glycerine and 60 per cent hot water to fill a suitable container about 10 cm/4 in deep. Stand the stems in the solution and leave in a cool dark place for about a week or until the colour changes.

Using desiccants

Flowers dried in desiccants such as borax, sand or silica gel retain their shape and colour beautifully, and this method is particularly suitable for flowers which would otherwise lose their shape while drying.

There are many desiccants you can use, but silica gel is the simplest and quickest. The crystals are bright blue when dry and change to pink when they absorb moisture, giving you the perfect indication of when your flowers are ready. Grind them down before use so that they are fine enough to fall between the flower petals. Other options include a mixture of equal parts silica gel with fine silver sand; one part sand to two parts borax; or three parts borax to one part table salt.

Choose a container which has a well fitting lid and which allows plenty of space for the flowers to be arranged without touching each other. It may be easier to dry flower heads in a shallow container then make wire stems when they are dry.

Fill the container with a layer of desiccant and sit the flower heads on top. Gradually cover them with the desiccant, making sure that it falls around and between the petals. Bell-shaped flowers, such as lily-of-the-valley, should be dried upside down, and you must cover them carefully so that the bells are filled with desiccant without misshaping them. Cover and seal the box and leave it for between two to five days until the flowers are dry and papery. Remove them and brush away the desiccant.

Pressing flowers

When pressing flowers, choose leaves or flowers which will look attractive when flat, or halve the flower or separate petals and press them individually.

Arrange the flowers between two sheets of blotting paper and lay them on a thick sheet of cardboard. You can then stack a number of layers together. Place them on a wooden base board and place a second board on top. Screw down the press or tie the boards securely and leave them for several months until completely dry.

the flowers and leaves are spread out. Hang them upside down from a pole across the ceiling. You may need to tighten the string as the stems shrink.

Grasses must be sprayed with hair lacquer or fixative before drying otherwise they will fall apart. They can be laid flat to dry on sheet of newspaper or cardboard. Lavender can also be dried in this way.

Tall grasses and seed heads such as pampas or bulrushes can be loosely arranged upright in an empty vase and left to dry. Other tall flowers such as delphinium or mimosa can be arranged in the same way with a little water in the bottom of the vase. The flowers absorb the water then gradually dry out.

Moss can be spread loosely in a box on a layer of newspaper and left to dry. Cones can be left in a basket or box to finish drying. Large flower heads need to be supported on a rack of chicken wire so that the stems can hang down.

January

'Lone flower, hemmed in with snows, and white as they

But hardier far, once more I see thee bend

Thy forehead as if fearful to offend,

Like an unbidden guest.'

William Wordsworth

January

When so many other plants are sleeping, this beautiful *Viburnum bodantense* 'Dawn' brightens the new year with its welcoming and wonderful displays of flowers, contrasting the vibrant colour of the blooms with the dark of the naked wood. For those who love colour in the garden, a winter-flowering viburnum is a perfect shrub to cultivate, giving you a succession of blooms to enliven the so-often dull months between December and February.

While it is easy to fill your garden with colour in the summer months, with a little thought and planning you can find hardy plants which will colour the shorter days of winter.

Colour for all seasons

A beautifully illustrated gardening book is something all flower-lovers should own. Not only will browsing through the pages give you hours of pleasure, enjoying the beauty of those perfect specimens and exotic species which may never grace your own garden, but you will certainly find it helpful in planning your garden so that you have a continuity of floral displays throughout the year.

1

2

Select your container carefully to suit the style of the flower arrangement. Large displays of shrubby material need a fairly heavy ceramic or terracotta pot.

3

4

Mahonia produces its vibrant yellow flowers early in the year. The glossy, spiky leaves can also be used in fresh flower arrangements, or they can be pressed or preserved in glycerine for dried displays. Some varieties, such as Mahonia japonica, *have wonderful russet leaves.*

5

Chinese flower arrangements traditionally include only one flower and this can be a stylish way to make good use of limited materials.

6

7

January

In winter, dried arrangements bring the life and colour to your rooms which may be lacking if you cannot obtain fresh flowers. Be adventurous when you are choosing materials and you will extend the range of possibilities open to you. Always be on the lookout for new ideas, whether you are pottering in your own garden, walking in the countryside or browsing round a craft shop.

In this arrangement, the strong shapes of the ornamental chillies stand out if you place the display in front of a window where the light can shine through the silvery honesty seed cases. The attractive curve of the drooping ears of wheat lends a grace, weight and balance.

Make a pretty garland of dried flowers to decorate your wall. Cut the flower stems short and wire them if necessary. Cover a dry foam ring with a base of filler material then arrange single flower heads all round until you have a pleasing and balanced display to finish with a pretty bow.

Tiny posies of dried flowers nestling in a doily collar and tied with a bow make a lovely gift or a table centre when filling a shallow basket.

Everlasting beauty

You should never need to run out of ideas for decorating your home with flowers if you make use of the wonderful range of dried materials available either from your garden or from the shops. If materials are limited, keep displays small and neat; if you have plenty of large flowers or grasses, go for a more imposing arrangement.

January

Jugs make useful flower containers, and those with a curvaceous form can help you to create wonderful, extravagantly-shaped displays of informal masses of flowers. For the most pleasing effects, keep the proportions of flowers to jug right, avoiding long stems. Here, Helleborus corsicus combines with variegated arum leaves and scented hyacinths to brighten the dullest winter day.

The various varieties of the hardy evergreen hellebores make lovely border plants, flowering even through the snows of Christmas and the New Year. The traditional Christmas rose is white but there are many varieties, and this superb Lenten rose, *Helleborus orientalis,* displays its rich speckled maroon flowers, delicately bowing their heads on slender, supple stems.

If you can resist the temptation to pick the flowers for the home, you will be rewarded with blooms that seem to last for many weeks, gradually being joined in the border by their less hardy neighbours.

Preserving Christmas roses

Even though they are long-lasting in the garden, you can preserve these beautiful flowers for even longer by drying them. The best method to use is to dry the flowers in a desiccant, wiring the stems afterwards for extra support if necessary. Since the petals lie quite flat, they are also suitable blooms for pressing to create framed pictures or crafted gifts.

15

16

17

18

19

Japanese orange trees, grown indoors in a container, make attractive decorations at this time of year.

20

21

January

Baskets lend themselves perfectly to dried flower arrangements, and this flat basket makes a delightful wall hanging.

Helichrysums provide the bright yellows and oranges for this arrangement, subtly interwoven with roses, nigella, carthamnus and rose leaves preserved in glycerine.

This type of display is best created by using a glue gun and short-stemmed flowers and leaves. Start by gluing some leaves across the front edge of the basket and over the handle. Then build up the rest of the design to give a pleasing balance and shape.

To make an attractive pressed-flower bookmark, cut a 20 x 8 cm/8 x 3 in piece of thick paper, score and fold it in half lengthways. Glue a loop of ribbon to the top and tails of ribbon to the bottom of one half. Glue an attractive design of pressed flower petals and leaves to the front using the whole length of the paper. Fold and glue the card together and cover with adhesive film.

Skeleton leaves

The intricate vein structure of evergreen leaves such as holly, magnolia or laurel can be exposed to blend delicately with dried flowers, provide an unusual contrast to evergreen or preserved leaves or to surround a posy instead of lace or a doily. Boil the leaves for 30 minutes in 600 ml/1 pt water with 100 g/4 oz biological detergent. Rinse, then brush away the leaf tissue from the central vein outwards using an old toothbrush. Rinse, dry and press between sheets of blotting paper for two weeks.

22

23

24

25

26

27

The earth in pot-grown flowering bulbs can be attractively covered with a layer of moss.

28

January

Towards the end of the winter, the florists have a greater range of flowers as the first hyacinths and ranunculuses come into bloom.

The garden, too, just begins to offer more choice, especially of foliage materials, hopefully including some variegated leaves which give such interest to an arrangement when combined with the glossy dark green of the evergreens.

The speckled heads of hellebores are still providing their delicate beauty and the winter-flowering viburnum adds a splash of colour and fragrance.

When using baskets for flower arranging, make sure they are tightly lined with plastic, or insert a plastic container hidden inside the basket and filled with moist foam.

Buy and borrow

Making the most of scarce materials
is an art in itself for the lover of
flowers. Supplement what you have
in your garden with flowers from the
florist, choosing carefully those
blooms which will complement your
own material. If you grow a
different selection of plants from
your neighbours, you can all benefit
by exchanging leaves, sprays or
flowers to grace your own displays.

*In the winter months, even the smallest
arrangement can give the greatest pleasure. A
few garden snowdrops look best displayed in a
tiny container which does not detract from
their fresh white and green.*

29

*As a simple guide to stylish flower arranging,
remember that the more an arrangement resembles the
growing plants, the more attractive it often is.*

30

31

February

Full many a gem of purest ray serene
The dark unfathomed caves of ocean bear:
Full many a flower is born to blush unseen,
And waste its sweetness on the desert air.'

Thomas Gray

February

The colours and beauty of the crocus is one of the first heralds of the coming spring, promising – at least to the optimists among us – warmer, sun-drenched days.

While the white, yellow and purples of the traditional varieties still retain their charm and beauty, new varieties are becoming available all the time with lovely shaped or veined petals, such as this stunning *Crocus chrysanthus* 'Gipsy girl' with its delicate feathering of tiger stripes.

For the most attractive displays, plant crocuses or other small flowers in clumps, grouping colour harmonies and contrasts and filling the garden with bright blooms.

Flowering through the grass

Especially if your lawn spreads beneath the shade of some trees, planting early spring bulbs beneath the lawn creates a wonderful display when the tiny pale buds push their way through the grass and burst into a riot of colour. If you like to cut your lawn early in the season, choose early-flowering crocuses rather than later daffodils so that you are not too impatient to cut them down after flowering.

The first spring flowers appear in the shops before your own garden flowers, and as they are usually cheap and plentiful they can provide a splash of bright colour and a welcome hint of spring even when the weather may still be cold.

1

2

3

4

*'Fair daffodils, we weep to see
You haste away so soon.'*
Robert Herrick

5

6

7

February

Heart-shaped baskets or ceramic containers are perfect for Valentine floral arrangements, whether to give as a gift or to decorate the table for a romantic candlelit dinner for two.

For a simple but stunning effect, choose just one or two flowers, such as these red roses framed with startling, fragrant, purple lilac blossom.

A softer and more delicate effect can be achieved by using a wider range of flowers, softly billowing from the heart-shaped container, in a subtler range of colours.

Victorian posies

There was nothing new, in Victorian times, in a posy being offered as a love token to a demure young lady. But it became fashionable for the posies to be tightly and formally arranged in circles of flowers, often surrounding a single rose bud, the symbol of young love. For the serious suitor, every chosen flower would convey a romantic meaning to his loved one – emotions he could not express in mere words.

8

9

10

Change in a trice! The lilies and languors of virtue
For the raptures and roses of vice.'

A.C. Swinburne

11

12

13

14

If the single red rose is not your style and a dozen long-stemmed roses are beyond your pocket, charm your valentine with a posy of roses, or other favourite flowers, surrounded with a delicate halo of gypsophilia, some ribbons or a collar of lace or doily.

February

The splendid and exotic orchid holds a fascination all its own. The vibrant colours and exciting petal forms and patterns can be almost unreal in their perfection and bring a feeling of tropical splendour. Although not a garden flower, orchids like these *Cymbidium* 'Aviemore' are not difficult to cultivate in a greenhouse and the display of flowers in February and March is worth the extra care they demand.

Orchids purchased from the florist tend to be expensive although they are very long-lasting. They are best displayed is very simple, oriental-style arrangements using just a few flowers in a tall, stylish vase so that you can enjoy the intricate beauty of the individual blooms.

Using the conservatory

For those seriously interested in orchid cultivation, a greenhouse is a necessity as you can create the ideal conditions for the flowers you wish to grow. However, with a little care you can offer similar conditions in a conservatory, and what a delight to be able to enjoy not only your familiar house plants but a few exotic and exquisite blooms.

15

16

*A single orchid makes a wonderful place decoration
at a special dinner party, or favour for your guests.*

17

18

19

20

*Tiny wild orchids can be found nestling in out of the
way corners. Enjoy them and leave them there - they
are protected.*

21

*Combine a limited number of exotic blooms,
such as orchids, with an interesting selection
of foliage. To make a low arrangement, tape
the foam to a shallow bowl. Beginning at the
bottom, build up a pyramid of foliage to cover
the base, then place the flowers tastefully
throughout the arrangement.*

February

*Make use of the variety of coloured irises
available in spring and combine them with
bright tulips for highlights of strong colour.
Background foliage can be kept to a
minimum, as with these long sprays of yew
and the ferny leaves of rue.*

Irises grow in many varieties and in such profusion you could have one in flower almost all the year. Ancient garden plants, they were cultivated in Asia well before the birth of Christ.

The little *Iris reticulata* springs from the earth with its wide-spread purple and yellow flowers stretching to greet the early spring sunshine. Other varieties, like the more unusual *Iris unguicularis,* thrive in undisturbed groups in a sunny dry spot and will flower throughout the winter months.

Smaller irises make a lovely addition to a pocket on a rockery, the front of a raised bed or a niche on a garden wall.

Indoors, these irises look very attractive grouped in pots and arranged in a shallow basket.

Floating iris

A few perfect blooms floating in a
shallow bowl is simplicity itself to
create but so effective as a
decoration on a side table or to
garnish each place at a dining table.
If you can, include a fragrant bloom
and a few scented lemon balm
leaves. Otherwise you can add a
little scented rose water or a drop of
pot pourri oil to the water.

22

23

*Spring catkins make a charming addition to flower
arrangements at this time of year.*

24

25

26

*An iris offers a lovely shape on which to base a
stencil design to print on a plain vase or on to
napkins, place mats or a table cloth.*

27

28/29

March

'I wandered lonely as a cloud
That floats on high o'er vales and hills,
When all at once I saw a crowd,
A host, of golden daffodils;
Beside the lake, beneath the trees,
Fluttering and dancing in the breeze.'

William Wordsworth

March

Add just a little imagination, and a table decoration using only a few simple flowers can be original and fun – and perfect for the children to make, too.

Clean egg shells, supported in a piece of egg box secured with Plasticine, make miniature containers for the tiny spring flowers, enveloped in a rustle of fresh hay. If you do not have an old nest, shape one from a handful of hay to contain a few sugar eggs and a tiny chick or two.

The flowers will not last very long, but will be sure to charm all your visitors.

Bursting out of the opening box with such enthusiasm, the faces of these bright little pansies look almost alive! To use such a container, simply place a plastic carton or several small jars inside the box, using foam, if necessary, to hold the flowers in place.

Edwardian pansy jelly

Dissolve 100 g/4 oz sugar in 450 ml/
¾ pt warm water and 150 ml/¼ pt
lemon juice with the thinly pared
rind of 2 lemons and ½ stick
cinnamon. Remove the cinnamon
and stir in 25 g/1 oz gelatine
dissolved in a little warm water. Beat
3 egg whites with 3 crushed egg
shells until frothy, add to the pan
with 6 tbsp sweet sherry and bring to
the boil, whisking. Cool until the
froth sinks. Boil and cool twice
more. Strain through muslin into
glasses and chill to set, reserving a
little jelly. Arrange pansy flowers on
top and cover with the reserved jelly.

*Sugar-sweet polyanthus combine well with the
buttery-scented grape hyacinth to make charming
spring arrangements.*

March

Spring bluebells look delightful with these delicate pale peach roses and carnations emerging from a mist of Queen Anne's lace. Early spring foliage, like this beech, is a wonderful vivid green – so fresh and alive.

Although the arrangement looks quite elaborate, it needs no mechanics since all the stems are self-supporting. Choose an attractive informal vase and start the arrangement at the back, creating the delicate arch of the final shape and gradually shortening the stems towards the front.

Remember to pick only bluebells you have grown in your garden, as wild flowers are best left alone to grace their woodland home.

Choose a firm, sound pumpkin, melon or squash, slice off the top and take a thin slice off the bottom so that it stands firm. Use a spoon to hollow out the inside, leaving a layer of flesh inside to keep it waterproof. Stand the container on a plate and fill with bright orange and yellow flowers.

8

9

One of the most delightfully scented spring flowers is the ever-popular lily-of-the-valley, a Victorian favourite which has never lost its appeal.

10

11

12

13

14

Unusual containers

Transform a plain ceramic vase with your own unique design. You can achieve a lovely natural effect using the ragging technique. Dip a small piece of cloth into some ceramic paint then blot it on to rough paper to remove excess paint. Press the rag gently round the vase, allowing the vase colour to show through. When the paint is dry, go over again with a second colour, or use a fine brush to splash brighter highlights over the surface.

March

Pot plants come in greater variety each year, and wonderful plants, such as *Clivia miniata*, are ideal for growing in the conservatory. The dark green, glossy leaves present a startling contrast to the clusters of orange-red flowers which can offer a succession of blooms from early spring to mid-summer.

Group your indoor plants in clusters at several heights, if possible, to give the best display, rather than standing them at evenly-spaced intervals around the window sills. You will find that it gives a much more pleasing effect, and it is also much easier to tend the plants when they are grouped together in one spot.

Contrast and complement

How you juxtapose your plants – whether in the garden, the conservatory or in a vase – is an art that is learned from experience and experiment. When you are working with flowers, try to envisage how the colour, texture and density of one plant's foliage, structure and bloom will look against its neighbours.

15

'And in green underwood and cover
Blossom by blossom the spring begins.'
A.C. Swinburne

16

17

18

19

20

21

Simple flower shapes lend themselves perfectly
as designs for the traditional art of quilling.
Cut strips of coloured paper 4 mm x 20 cm /
³⁄₁₆ x 8 in. Coil them tightly then release the
coil so it springs open slightly and glue the end
against one side. Draw your outline design
on a card or the top of a box and glue on the
coils a section at a time, gently pressing them
into shape as you do so.

March

A stone wall or a grassy bank offer the perfect spot for purple aubretia, yellow or white alyssum, blue lobelia, violets or clumps of mauve thrift. The mounting cascades of bloom can cover an unattractive wall, or complement the beauty of natural stone peeping out between the flowers.

For added interest when the plants are not in flower, some varieties of aubretia have attractive variegated leaves which enliven not only the garden but also delicate floral arrangements for the home.

Clumps of chives with their baubles of lilac-pink flowers grow well on the top of a rockery wall as long as the soil is fairly moist.

Violet honey

Take a step back into Victorian times and spread your home-made scones with flower-scented honey. Stir half a cup of washed violet petals into half a jar of honey, cover and stand the jar on a trivet or cloth in a saucepan. Fill with water to the neck of the jar, bring to the boil and simmer for 30 minutes. Remove the jar from the pan and leave to cool then infuse for 7 days. Warm the jar of honey then strain the honey into a clean jar.

Originally woodland flowers, Anemone nemorosa are now cultivated in gardens and look beautiful planted around trees or in rock gardens. The fine white petals of 'Vestal' are surrounded by a crown of larger petals.

22

23

24

25

26

27

The pink-flowered bergenia got its nickname 'elephants' ears' from its large, glossy, leathery leaves which spread across the soil.

28

March

ising from a mass of purple pansies which serve to emphasise their tall and stately stems, these lovely pink tulips show of their best against the soft grey of the stone wall behind.

Because of the stiff style of their blooms, tulips always look best planted among other, lower-growing flowers, or in tight clumps which make the best display of their clean, vibrant colours.

Experiment in the garden when planting to find happy associations of plants, creating unusual and surprising combinations which give renewed delight in favourite plants.

Tulips and lilac

Happily, tulips bloom at the same time as the lilac, for in floral arrangements they were made for each other, providing a delicate balance of fragrance and a beautiful combination of the simple outlines of the tulip with the frothy exuberance of the lilac florets.

29

'In the late seventeenth century, tulips were very popular and blue and white Delftware pyramid vases were imported specially from Holland.

30

31

Use heavy craft paper to cut six petals and two leaves for a paper tulip. Colour the petals delicately pink at the top edge then stretch them into a cup shape. Cover the end of a stub wire with a roll of green paper. Cut one edge of a strip of black crêpe into narrow strips and twist six to make stamens to fix around the centre. Wire on the petals in two layers then wind a ribbon of crêpe to cover the stem, attaching the leaves at the base.

April

'From you have I been absent in the spring,

When proud-pied April, dressed in all his trim,

Hath put a spirit of youth in every thing.'

William Shakespeare

April

Pick dry, sweetly-scented elderflowers in full sun to make a delicious wine; avoid flowers that smell unpleasant.

Place the florets from 3 large elderflower heads in a bucket with 2.5 l/5 pts boiling water. Cover and leave for 2 days, stirring regularly. Boil 1 kg/2 lb sugar and 600 ml/1pt water, cool slightly, mix in 1 packet wine yeast then pour into a demijohn.

Strain and discard the flowers. To the water, add 150 ml/¼ pt white grape juice concentrate, 1 tsp citric acid, 1 tsp yeast nutrient and a cup of strong tea. Pour into the demijohn, top up with water and shake well. Fit an airlock and leave in a warm place, shaking daily until fermentation has stopped. Siphon into a clean jar, top up with apple juice, add a crushed Campden tablet and refit the airlock. Leave in a cool place for 9 to 12 months, siphoning every 3 months.

To make elderflower cleansing cream, simmer 300 ml/½ pt yoghurt and the flowers from 2 large elderflower heads gently for 30 minutes then cover and set aside for 3 hours. Strain, stir in 3 tbsp honey and whisk until thick. Pour into jars, label and store in the refrigerator.

Elderflower milk shake

For a drink full of protein, vitamins and flavour, heat 600 ml/1pt buttermilk with 3 large elderflower heads and 2 tbsp honey almost to boiling. Cool and strain through a coffee filter. Blend with 2 egg yolks then fold in 2 whisked egg whites. Pour into glasses, top with a spoonful of yoghurt and sprinkle with cinnamon.

Pour a little boiling water on some elderflower heads, leave to cool, then strain the perfumed water into ice cube trays to make elderflower ice cubes.

April

The delicate, bell-shaped flowers of *Frittilaria meleagris* droop gently on their tender stems. Although some varieties only grow in greenhouses in temperate areas, this favourite of woodland and river bank will bloom in a quiet spot in most borders.

The name derives from *fritillus*, or dice-box, which the flower was supposed to resemble in its markings.

For a particularly charming display, try the old-fashioned habit of growing them with some forget-me-nots to give a lovely contrast between the clear blue of those ever-popular plants and the purple chequerboard of the snake's head fritillary.

Orchids are perfect for wide displays. Fix foam in a shallow container. Create the shape for the base of the arrangement with foliage then add two gracefully-drooping stems of flowers and a few flower heads at the front to give a delicately undulating curve. Give height with a few erect stems of flowers and a little attractive greenery.

Witches used to make potions from orchid tubers - they were believed to have aphrodisiac qualities.

Medicinal flowers

Plants which resembled particular parts of the body were often thought to be of benefit to that part and were used in medicines. Because it looked like eyes, eyebright was thought to be good for the eyes, the shape of liverwort meant that it must benefit the liver and the lung-like pattern on pulmonaria led to it being prescribed for respiratory problems.

April

It is wonderful to plant your garden with a few fruit trees, and this is no longer difficult even for those with smaller gardens as there are many dwarf varieties or varieties which can be grown against a suitable wall or even across a pergola.

As well as yielding fruit, they can make lovely displays of blossom to lighten your garden in the spring.

Apple blossom is extremely versatile. It makes a lovely wine, especially with apple and orange juices. The flowers can be pressed for crafts or can be used to make flower oils, flower syrup (May 1), soap (May 22) or other cosmetics.

Magnolia blossoms burst from the dark, leafless twigs in May, filling sheltered spots in the garden with their rich fragrance. An ancient plant, the magnolia bears a strong resemblance to the first plants that appeared some 135 million years ago.

Flower oils

It is not as easy to make flower oils as it is to buy them, but it can be fun. Pick 10 large cupfuls of fragrant petals. Heat 300 ml/½ pt almond oil in the top of a double boiler and stir in 2 cups of petals. Cover tightly and leave on a low heat for 2 hours. Strain, reserving the flowers. Add fresh flowers and repeat until you have used all the flowers. Pour the oil and all the flowers into a pan and simmer over a low heat for 1 hour or until the flowers are dry. Press the oil through muslin or a sieve. Stir in 1 tsp each liquid storax and tincture benzoin, bottle, seal, label and store in a dry, dark place.

15

16

17

*A vase of magnolia buds arranged in the evening
will open during the night to scent a whole room.*

18

19

*You can create the simplest arrangement with a few
sprays of apple blossom dotted with spring bluebells.*

20

21

April

Many plant species have been brought to Western shores from the Orient, and the beautiful spring-flowering *Kerria japonica* is one which originated in China and remains popular both there and in neighbouring Japan.

The first plants to be introduced to other countries had delicate, buttercup-like single flowers in the familiar rich yellow-orange. Now we are more likely to recognise the frothy double yellow flowers which cluster together to soak up the warming sun, almost obliterating the pretty, serrated leaves behind. In Victorian gardens, they were often grown to cover walls or fences, a task which they fulfil admirably.

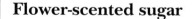

Flower-scented sugar

Mix some washed and dried petals of marigold or other fragrant flowers with twice their volume of sugar. Spread the mixture on baking trays and place in the oven at the lowest setting for about 2 hours, turning frequently until the sugar has absorbed the moisture from the petals and dried. Cool, sieve and store in a cool, dry place.

22

23

24

25

26

27

Flower arrangements always stay fresher if positioned in a cool place away from direct sun and where they are not disturbed as people pass.

28

In spring, there is always an abundance of bright yellow and orange flowers which work so well together. Always start by arranging your background foliage to create the size and shape you want, then add each type of bloom one at a time, spaced evenly through the arrangement.

April

Native to Japan and Korea, the exotic *Camellia japonica* was first grown in conservatories when it was brought to the West in the seventeenth century as it was thought to be very tender.

Although the many varieties now growing in our gardens proves that this was unnecessary, the plants do have quite specific needs which must be catered for if they are to provide the wonderful displays of familiar, rose-like flowers. The blooms can be found in many colours and patterns of such perfection that the flower came to be associated with loveliness and excellence.

Using foliage

As well as boasting such splendid blooms, the dark, glossy camellia foliage can add depth and contrast to your flower arrangements in the home.

When choosing foliage, make sure that it blends with the style of flowers you are using: delicate wispy or silvery leaves with smaller subtle flowers, or firmer, larger leaves for bigger blooms.

29

30

Using a wooden frame from a craft shop, you
can create pretty pressed flower pictures with
camellias, roses or other blooms. Cut white or
suitably-coloured card to fit the frame and
a mount from thin card. Mark the area inside
the mount on the white card. Recreate the flower
in pressed petals, glueing with latex adhesive. Place
the mount over the top, cover with the glass and
mount into the frame.

May

'Mid-May's eldest child,
The coming musk-rose, full of dewy wine,
The murmurous haunt of flies on summer eves.'

John Keats

May

The glorious freshness and fragrance of the May blossom smothering the spring-green hedgerows is a sure sign that warmer weather is on the way.

For those who love to harvest the hedgerows, the hawthorn must be one of their favourite plants, for the flowers can be used for cosmetics or to make dry white wine, and the small, fan-shaped leaves, picked in their prime, are delicious in salads.

Toss 2 handfuls of young hawthorn leaves with a handful each of young dandelion leaves and hedge garlic leaves, a cup of broom buds and 2 sliced spring onions. Toss the salad with a dressing made from 4 tbsp olive oil, 1 tbsp orange juice, 2 tsp honey and a few drops of soy sauce and season with salt and pepper.

Mayflower syrup

Fragrant flower syrup is delicious for dressing fruit salad, for poaching fruit or in baked puddings. Place 450 g/1 lb sugar, 300 ml/½ pt water and 1 cup of fragrant petals in a saucepan and heat gently, stirring to dissolve the sugar. Bring to the boil then simmer for 10 minutes. Cool, strain and bottle. Store in the refrigerator for 2 weeks or sterilise the bottles by placing on a trivet in a saucepan of water and boiling for 10 minutes.

1

2

3

4

5

When the hawthorn berries appear later in the year, they can be used for making jelly or mixed fruit jam and for flavouring liqueurs.

6

7

As the lush and varied greens of the herb garden are coming to their best, make an arrangement in a plastic-lined basket of herbs such as rue, mint, dill, borage, rosemary and chives. A small container is best as you can use it to create a dense hummock of foliage and flowers.

May

Dandelion wine is a favourite of home wine-makers. Discard all the green parts from 3.4 l/6pts dandelion flowers and put the petals in a muslin bag with the finely pared rind of 1 orange and 1 lemon. Secure the bag and place in a saucepan with 4.5 l/8pts water, bring to the boil and simmer for 20 minutes. Squeeze the bag to remove the liquid, then discard the petals.

Pour the liquid into a bucket and stir in 1.5 kg/3 lb sugar, the juice of the orange and lemon and 1 cup of strong black tea. Mix a packet of wine yeast with a little warm water and leave for 5 minutes then stir it into the bucket. Cover and leave for 5 days, stirring daily.

Siphon into a demijohn, seal with an airlock and leave for about 3 months until fermentation has finished. Siphon into bottles and store for several months before drinking.

Craft shops sell plain cork drinks coasters which look wonderful decorated with dried flowers. Make sure the coasters are slightly larger than the base of your glasses. Glue helichrysum or other small flower heads carefully around the edge and leave to dry thoroughly before using.

Flower wines

Many wines can be made using flower petals such as hawthorn, lime blossom, lemon thyme, rose petal, primrose, honeysuckle, broom, wallflower or even gorse – if you have the patience and thick skin to pick the blossom! They usually make light, delicately-scented table wines. Unless you are experienced at home wine-making, it is a good idea to follow the recipe quite closely with regard to the quantity of flowers so that the bouquet is not overpowering.

8

9

10

11

12

The traditional day for picking the first dandelions is St George's Day on April 23.

13

14

May

 favourite of the Edwardians, the *Aquilegia vulgaris* remains popular in many gardens for its delicate funnel-shaped flowers in pinks, purples and blues which rise from the foliage on tall stems. Its old-fashioned name, granny's bonnet, is now rarely used although it is wonderfully descriptive of these charming, delicate flowers.

Another common name for the plant is columbine, and many will recognise this name more readily, for it was also popular with the Elizabethans and raises its pretty head in many a poem.

Although they make a wonderful addition to stylish flower arrangements, they are not very long-lived so must be treated carefully.

When arranging with small, delicate flowers, you can often use tiny, unusual containers. Tape a little foam into a large scallop shell to make an arrangement of short-stemmed aquilegia, forget-me-nots or pansies.

The Mexican lily

From Mexico and South American, *Ipheion uniflorum* is an unusual but beautiful visitor to European gardens, brightening rock gardens with its star-shaped flowers.

The pale green leaves, long and narrow, have a faintly garlic smell.

15

16

17

18

19

20

*Glass marbles in a plain glass vase look very
attractive and help to hold flower stems in place.*

21

May

The colourful tangle of the traditional cottage garden has never lost its popularity, and the favourite old-fashioned flowers are often best suited to such wonderful carefree masses of blooms such as these wallflowers and forget-me-nots.

Although many varieties have now been overbred and lost their original fragrances, scented flowers are again becoming more popular, and the wallflower is one of the best to choose.

Fragrant soap

Put 300 ml/½ pt water in a glass (not metal) bowl and stir in 4 tbsp caustic soda with a wooden spoon. Warm 3 tbsp each coconut, sunflower and olive oil until the same temperature as the soda, which will have heated spontaneously. Pour the oil into the soda, stirring constantly. Add a few drops each of food colouring and fragrant oil (Apr 15) and beat until thick and opaque. Quickly pour into moulds such as small bowls, jelly moulds or yoghurt pots, stand on a cooling rack and leave in a warm, dry place for 24 hours until set. Remove from the moulds, wrap in greaseproof paper and leave for 3 weeks to harden.

If you choose a low container, the flowers in a cottage-style arrangement will support each other without any additional mechanics. Here the warmth of rich apricot roses and spray carnations contrasts with the acid lime green of euphorbia and guelder rose blossoms, cooled with sprays of fragrant white lilac.

It used to be popular to grow some attractive vegetables in the flower border for variety and interest.

May

The Greek name rhododendron means rose tree, and the plant was first introduced into Europe in the seventeenth century. Although often separated, it is in fact the same genus as the azalea.

We have the aristocratic love of rhododendrons and azaleas to thank for so many old-established displays of these stunning and often strikingly-fragrant plants.

They were often planted as screens and hedges on country estates, fulfilling that task admirably with the added advantage of their lovely blooms in May and June.

In Windsor, in England, the Royal estates boast many wonderful rhododendrons and azaleas which now delight visitors as much as they once delighted their Royal owners.

A garden indoors

In the Victorian era, even large rhododendrons were brought into the great houses to decorate the hall or the rooms for banquets or weekend gatherings. Once the event was over, or the plant became too massive, the gardener planted it out into the grounds.

29

30

31

An open fireplace in summer demands a lavish flower arrangement, especially for a special occasion. The variety of different flowers in this arrangement – including gerbera, lilies and irises – are styled and structured by their shape and colour. Tape a large piece of foam securely to a waterproof base and soak it thoroughly. Flowers which are to be seen from above, especially large arrangements, are best arranged in situ.

June

'O, my Luve's like a red red rose
That's newly sprung in June:
O, my Luve's like the melodie
That's sweetly play'd in tune.'

Robert Burns

June

These beautiful rambling roses provide the perfect frame for this cottage window, tumbling round and almost spilling into the room. Roses and honeysuckle are particularly popular to grow on a trellis on a house wall so that you can enjoy their beauty and fragrance inside and out.

The arrangement of orange and yellow flowers inside give a wonderful, vibrant effect against the dark furniture. Strong colours can be difficult to arrange successfully, but here the bright orange of lilies and marigolds is tempered by plenty of white feverfew flowers and masses of green foliage.

Flowering through the summer

When planting in boxes or tubs, or near the house, make sure you plan the plants to give a succession of flowers for as much of the year as possible.

If all your flowers bloom together in the spring, you will have nothing to look forward to and enjoy for the rest of the summer.

Window boxes, hanging baskets and hollow walls can transform an ordinary small garden into a riot of colour. Make drain holes in the window box and cover the base with crocks before filling with a suitable compost. Pelargoniums, petunias, alyssum, lobelia, nemesia, all thrive in boxes and tubs if watered and trimmed regularly.

1

One of the best plants for attracting butterflies is the scented buddleia.

2

3

4

5

6

7

June

Pergolas and arches

Even in a small garden, a climbing rose or other flower trained up a pergola adds a touch of cottage style.

This cascading arch of laburnum, dripping sunshine, has been tended for many years at Barnsley House in Gloucestershire, England.

Most of us do not have the space for such an ambitious project, but the laburnum is nonetheless an easy tree to grow in most gardens. It provides a welcome early display of lovely pendulous flowers which are quite long-lasting in the garden, and can also be used to give a graceful shape to large arrangements.

The ever-popular lupin is often the children's favourite in the garden, especially when the tall spires of flowers transform into those wonderfully-soft seed cases.

When so many gardens and flower beds are square or rectangular, adding a carefully placed arch can help you to establish a more curvaceous and sweeping design.

It can also help to give the impression of a larger garden as the viewer is offered only glimpses of what lies beyond the floral rainbow.

Flowers and herb clippings from Tudor herb gardens were strewn on the floors with the rushes to impart their delicate aroma to the house.

Keep your herb garden tidy and encourage fresh growth by trimming herbs regularly for use in the kitchen.

June

Not only is it popular with crossword-compilers and in spelling tests, the chrysanthemum must be one of the most numerous flowers in our gardens, with literally hundreds of varieties from which to choose.

Almost every shade of red, pink, white, orange and yellow is represented in blooms ranging from small and flat to large, round and exuberant. Varieties flower through the summer and into the autumn, and are perfect for simple flower arrangements.

Minted face mask

Although you must take care that it does not overrun less robust plants, mint looks attractive in the flower border and has more uses than just to flavour the potatoes.

Simmer 4 tbsp each finely chopped mint and water for 5 minutes. Remove from the heat and stir in 1 tbsp clear honey, 2 tbsp fine oatmeal and 3 tbsp milk. Cool, then apply evenly over the face, avoiding the eyes, rest for 30 minutes then rinse.

Peonies are magnificent flowers to grace the early summer garden although, sadly, for such a short time. Make the most of them while they are in flower or dry them when they are just opening out from the bud stage.

15

If you like to sit in your garden in the evening, plant some night-scented stocks or other flowers which release their fragrance at the end of the day.

16

17

18

19

20

Very brightly coloured arrangements were favourites of the early Victorians, who loved to mix startling colours and patterns.

21

June

The drooping racemes of lovely wisteria flowers could not be more attractively positioned than hanging elegantly from the wall of this delightful country cottage.

Originally from Japan and China, the delicate lilac blossoms reflect the understated elegance of the East, while the gnarled and flaking trunk calls bonsai to mind.

One of the most popular of climbing plants, it is not difficult to grow, once established, but does need support and benefits from cutting back after flowering.

Honeysuckle for the bees

Honeysuckle, like this *Lonicera x tellmanniana,* is another delightful plant which clambers up walls, round pergolas or along hedges, scenting the air with the wonderful perfume of its early summer flowers. Watch the bees swarm to it when the flowers are at their peak.

Grow it with an ivy for an attractive combination.

This romantic corsage
for a wedding guest makes
use of honeysuckle, sweet peas, pale
pink roses and white miniature gladioli.
Group the flowers attractively so that
the stems are covered by the blooms.
Wire them together and bind
the stems with ribbon or tape.

Some of the old-fashioned climbing roses are again
becoming available and these often combine beauty
with wonderful, almost-forgotten fragrances.

In the right spot, clematis will grow profusely to cover
an unattractive fence or wall.

June

Plan your hanging baskets early in the season so that you can enjoy the beauty of the flowers at the earliest opportunity.

Try to strike a balance between not overcrowding the plants too much when you prepare the basket – so that they have plenty of space to grow – and being too meagre in your selection. Remember that one of the joys of such a display is the overflowing exuberance of the blooms, so it is probably better to err on the side of generosity.

Thyme is another pretty herb which can be basket or pot grown before transplanting into the herb garden.

To put together a hanging basket, line the basket with moss, foam or a liner. Half fill with compost then gradually introduce the chosen plants, filling with compost and firming down as you do so, and positioning them so that the trailing plants are at the edge and the tallest plants in the centre.

Herbs in the basket

Including a herb such as a small rosemary plant in your selection of plants for hanging baskets gives you subtle leaf colour as well as pretty flowers sporadically throughout the season.

At the end of the season, the rosemary can be planted into the garden and will grace the border or herb garden for many years and provide fresh aromatic herbs for the kitchen.

July

'I know a bank whereon the wild thyme blows,
Where oxlips and the nodding violet grows
Quite over-canopied with luscious woodbine,
With sweet musk-roses, and with eglantine.'

William Shakespeare

July

Although their flowering season is often shorter than the modern shrub roses, the old roses have a character and beauty all their own, enhanced by their wonderful perfumes. Subtle pinks and rose-blushed whites are the favourite colours for these blooms.

'Fantin Latour' is an immensely popular old rose with cup-shaped, warm pink double flowers which bloom in mid-summer.

Rose pot pourri

Make your own rose pot pourri. Mix 8 cups of dried, fragrant rose petals with 1 tbsp ground cloves, 2 tbsp each ground allspice, ground cinnamon and ground orris and a few drops of rose oil.

Store in a sealed container for 6 weeks before arranging in open bowls or pot pourri containers.

Roses, gladioli and lilies combine to make a classically-simple bridal bouquet. The flowers only need to be individually wired if the stems are too clumsy to make a neat handle. If they are wired, cover them neatly with gutta-percha tape or ribbon.

1

At Ancient Roman assemblies, the floors would be strewn with rose petals to impart their delicate perfume to the gathering.

2

3

4

5

6

7

July

Tall flowers can dwarf other blooms in the garden if not carefully positioned, while at the back of a cottage-style flower border they will provide depth to the flower bed and a wonderful backdrop for the smaller flowers in front.

Delphiniums are not only splendid in the garden, but also provide lovely cut flowers for tall arrangements in the home. The dusty blue of these 'Dora Larkin' are typical of the colour range: blues, purples and whites predominating. Although recent experimental breeding has introduced shades of red and yellow, the traditional delphinium blue will never be replaced.

It is hard to believe that the rich blooms of Ranunculus asiaticus *have anything to do with the common buttercup, but they are related. Although not frequently grown in gardens, these flowers are freely available from the florist and are wonderful for any style of arrangement.*

Foxgloves and fennel

Old woodland foxgloves can look very attractive in the border, especially if grown in dappled shade under the trees.

Arranged with the feathery foliage of fennel, they look particularly attractive in the home.

And I wove the thing to a random rhyme,
For the Rose is Beauty, the Gardener, Time.'
Austin Dobson

'Cornflower blue' is a favourite description and
nothing else quite evokes the wonderful colour of these
delightful flowers.

July

Marigolds and nasturtiums can also be used to make an attractive country-style summer wreath. *The flowers of* Alchemilla mollis *provide a welcome frivolity while golden marjoram leaves add a note of bright green and a sweet herbal scent. Cover a foam ring with foliage before spacing the flowers around the circle.*

The most beautiful salad you can imagine – and the most delicious – may be just waiting in your garden. Marigolds, nasturtiums and borage flowers mixed with a few salad leaves and a little fresh mint and dill taste superb for a summer lunch table.

What's more, you can decorate the table with the same ingredients, as this charming little pom-pom of nasturtium flowers and parsley so clearly shows.

15

16

Scatter a few flower heads over an arrangement of colourful fruit or vegetables as a novel table centre.

17

18

19

Freshly grown parsley

Parsley is too well known to demand a description and grows in rounded mounds of foliage throughout the summer. It will thrive in moist, reasonably-fertile soils in sun or partial shade. If your soil is very poor or dry, you may be more successful growing parsley in a pot or window box so that you have a constant and accessible supply both for the kitchen and small flower arrangements.

20

Never use plants for culinary purposes unless you know exactly what they are and that they are safely edible.

21

July

Even the humblest of containers and simple garden flowers can make a stunning arrangement to grace your home. Informal and loosely arranged, this tumble of flowers will brighten any room.

Choosing a limited range of colour lends style to an arrangement. Here, the subtle coral pinks of the roses and honeysuckle beautifully complement the dusty green of the homely jug.

Start by filling the jug with water and arranging stems of honeysuckle of equal length. Next place roses with stems of equal length throughout the arrangement, letting some of them fall naturally over the edge to lend movement. A single stem of honeysuckle and a pretty ornament finish the display.

A carefully chosen mixture of pink flowers makes a delightful posy to give as a gift. The coral rose centrepiece is surrounded by purple sage, London Pride, spikes of polygonum and lovely pelargonium flowers. Twist a doily round the back of the posy and secure it with tape for an attractive finishing effect.

Fragrant summer flowers

Roses and honeysuckle are among the most fragrant flowers to grow in your garden. Many other favourite old-fashioned flowers also have wonderful fragrances: wallflowers, buddleia, pinks, freesias, gardenia, sweet peas, lilac, roses and viburnum. Not all modern varieties are scented, however, so make sure that you plant a scented variety.

22

23

24

25

26

27

Bowls of fragrant rose petals will impart their wonderful scent to your room.

28

July

Philadelphus 'Boule d'Argent' is one of many varieties of the mock orange shrub, so called because the strong fragrance of the flowers is reminiscent of orange blossom. Some flowers are double, some single, and a few have a purple tinge to the base of the flower.

Because they are strong and woody, philadelphus work best in large floral arrangements and are perfect for fireplace displays or impressive stands of flowers.

Carefully-placed tubs of flowers can be used to blur the edge of a patio, path or border and give a real feeling of exuberance in the garden. Always position tubs before planting. Cover drain holes with crocks and fill with a suitable compost before planting and watering thoroughly.

Flowering shrubs

Especially for the gardener who is short of time to lavish on more tender varieties, flowering shrubs can be a great boon in the garden, providing colour and beauty with the minimum of effort. As well as philadelphus, buddleia, gardenia, forsythia, senecio and cotoneaster are all popular with busy gardeners. Hydrangea is particularly useful for the flower-lover as the flower heads can be dried for attractive winter arrangements.

Garlands of exotic flowers have long been used as a welcoming gift to visitors to the Pacific Islands.

August

'To set budding more,
And still more, later flowers for the bees,
Until they think warm days will never cease,
For Summer has o'erbrimmed their clammy
cells.'

John Keats

August

A 1950s lustre bowl sponged with a pink design below the gold rim makes an ideal container for a large bunch of sugar-pink roses and paler pink spray carnations. The grey-green foliage of eucalyptus is the perfect foil.

Roses will adapt to almost any style of arrangement, from a formal display to a simple handful of pretty summer flowers on the kitchen table.

Miniature roses

For low borders or in tubs on the patio, miniature roses make an attractive display to bloom through the summer.

For a charming birthday or anniversary gift, offer a potted miniature rose in a pretty basket or container.

There is no need to be limited by the range in your garden since they are available all year round from the florist or nursery.

1

If you are travelling with flowers – a bouquet for a gift or a corsage for a wedding – place them in a cool box and they will arrive in perfect condition.

2

3

4

5

6

7

What can equal the beauty of a perfect rose like this 'Australian gold'? Since there are almost too many from which to choose, it can sometimes be difficult to buy roses for the garden. Ask the nurseryman's advice on which will grow best in your type of soil rather than simply deciding on the basis of colour or scent and being disappointed by poor results.

August

The frilled delicacy of this fuchsia 'Lovely' would enhance any garden. Extremely versatile, fuchsia varieties can be grown as bushes or standards, planted in hanging baskets, tubs or window boxes. Some need protection during the colder months, but others are hardy and can simply be cut back when they are finished at the end of the season and left until they re-emerge the following year.

Many fuchsias flower late in the season and will continue to bloom until the nights become quite cold.

Hanging baskets

Trailing fuchsias are perfect for hanging baskets as they provide a succession of colourful flowers which will hang over the edge of the basket. Mix them with lobelia, pelargoniums or petunias, or add some ivy which will trail down with the colourful blooms.

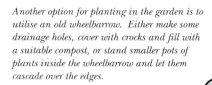

Another option for planting in the garden is to utilise an old wheelbarrow. Either make some drainage holes, cover with crocks and fill with a suitable compost, or stand smaller pots of plants inside the wheelbarrow and let them cascade over the edges.

Smaller herbs such as marjoram or thyme grow well in tubs or window boxes.

A white-painted tyre can make an interesting little raised flower bed for summer-blooming flowers or herbs.

August

At the back of the flower bed, against a warm, sunny fence or wall, is the place for the sunflowers in your garden. The traditional yellow-headed *Helianthus annuus is* the children's favourite, but you may prefer a variety such as this 'Autumn Beauty' with its rich russet petals.

When the flower heads go to seed, they have a rugged autumnal beauty of their own, and can be used in impressive dried arrangements.

You can also save the seeds – some to plant for next year, some to feed the birds and some for your own kitchen.

Straw flowers

The beautiful helichrysum, or straw flower, is a favourite of all those who enjoy arranging dried flowers because it grows almost ready-dried, with a spiky and straw-like texture.

It flowers in a range of colours and brightens any flower border.

15

16

17

18

19

20

21

This lovely bridesmaid's basket and circlet displays the rich colours of late summer. To keep the flowers fresh, line the basket with plastic and press the flowers into a piece of securely-fixed foam. Deep coral spray carnations have been wired into a circlet with creamy yellow freesias and gypsophilia.

Many montbresias like similar conditions to sunflowers and are perfect for growing in front of them in the border.

August

One of the oldest cultivated flowers, the lily has been cherished for at least 3,000 years in Ancient Egypt, Rome, Greece, China and Japan. For centuries, only a few species were known, such as the white madonna lily, but now that the lily has been developed commercially, its popularity is set to continue.

The lily has a unique perfection among the flowers and, like the rose, has always been seen as a symbolic flower. The white lily has long represented purity, and the regal lily, majesty.

Lilies can be massed together in mixed borders, placed among shrubs and on large rock gardens, or grown as pot plants. Several are suitable for a wild or woodland garden. Only a few tender species require greenhouse cultivation.

Stargazer lilies

Nothing could be simpler than a tall glass vase used to display several stems of the exquisite and highly scented lily 'Stargazer'. The lilies arrange themselves as the stems fall into place.

Water lilies like this beautiful Nymphaea alba *make the most stunning pond flowers. When planting, trim off any old brown roots and plant in a plastic container lined with hessian and partly filled with loam. Top-dress with shingle to stop any fish uprooting the plants. Position in the pool so that the shingle is just below the water surface.*

22

23

Spring-blooming lilies are the traditional choice for Church altar flower arrangements at Easter.

24

25

26

Float lily heads in a shallow glass bowl for an instant table decoration.

27

28

August

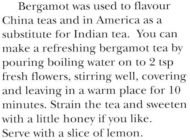

ess popular now than a century ago, both in gardens and in the kitchen, the pretty bergamot, *Monarda didyma*, deserves its place in herb garden or flower border for its startling, hooked, scarlet flowers. It thrives in a moist soil with not too much sun and, being a showy individual, spreads boldly in its own space without being overshadowed by other plants.

Bergamot was used to flavour China teas and in America as a substitute for Indian tea. You can make a refreshing bergamot tea by pouring boiling water on to 2 tsp fresh flowers, stirring well, covering and leaving in a warm place for 10 minutes. Strain the tea and sweeten with a little honey if you like. Serve with a slice of lemon.

Sage shampoo

Sage shampoo is ideal for dark hair. For fair hair, use camomile flowers or for red hair, marigold petals.

Pour 1.5 1/2½ pts boiling water over 1 cup of sage leaves, stir, cover and leave to stand for 2 hours. Strain the liquid through a sieve, pressing to extract all the fragrance. Add 6 tbsp grated castile soap and whisk over a low heat until the soap has dissolved. Cool, bottle and label. Shake the bottle well before use and rinse your hair thoroughly after shampooing.

29

Freeze borage flowers in ice cubes to garnish summer drinks.

30

31

Collect several different varieties of herbs, including some in flower, and group them into a posy, trimming the stems to the same length. Hold them together with an elastic band and cover with a ribbon.

September

'Here are sweet-peas, on tip-toe for a flight:
With wings of gentle flush o'er delicate white,
And taper fingers catching at all things,
To bind them all about with tiny rings.'

John Keats

September

 ou can make your pot pourri baskets as pretty as any floral arrangement. This Victorian basket is filled with a pot pourri made from rose petals and summer flowers.

To make the whole thing more decorative, dried flower heads have been wired around the edge of the basket. Pink peonies, helichrysums, delphinium and bronzy-cream hydrangea florets make the perfect materials for the flowery edges.

Lemon pot pourri

Try different recipes when making your pot pourri. For a freshly scented yellow mixture, combine 1 cup each of dried forsythia and camomile flowers, 1 cup each of dried lemon verbena and lemon balm leaves and 1 cup of dried marigold petals. Stir in the thinly pared rind of a lemon and 3 tbsp ground orris. Cover and leave in a warm, dry place for 6 weeks. Stir in 5 or 6 drops of lemon verbena oil to complete.

These little pot pourri bags make delightful gifts. Cut a 30 cm/12 in diameter circle from a piece of pretty fabric, fold back and hem the edge and run a gathering thread a little way in from the edge, leaving the ends trailing. Fill the bag with pot pourri, draw up and secure. Use ribbon or a length of fabric, folded and stitched, to make a handle and sew this on to the bag. Decorate the top with ribbon or a circlet of wired dried flowers.

1

2

3

Layer coloured pot pourri in an attractive glass jar, cover with lace and tie with a pretty ribbon.

4

5

6

Maintain the fragrance of your pot pourri by adding a few drops of refresher oil occasionally and stirring it into the petals.

7

September

Plants which flower abundantly in late summer, when so many others are fading and beginning to hide away in preparation for the colder months to come, are a delight.

The rich purple spires of this loosestrife, *Lythrum salicaria*, flood the borders with a mass of colour from the tiny, star-shaped flowers borne in profusion on the spire-like racemes.

Wild Beauty

Some of the most charming flowers we remember from our childhood are the wild flowers: poppies, dog roses, nightshade – even the humble buttercups and daisies. Happily many are returning to the hedgerows as farmers cease to flood the land with chemicals. You can also keep a wild flower corner in your own garden.

8

9

10

Asters flower late in the season, hence the popular name of the most famous one, the Michaelmas daisy.

The beautiful red-orange flowers of this trumpet vine, Campsis x tagliabuana *'Madame Gallen', appear in August and September. The plant is usually grown on walls, fences or pergolas as it is self-clinging. The flowers excellent for cutting or arrangements.*

11

12

13

14

September

When the flowers have long gone, you can still enjoy the russet rose hips gathering and swelling on the hedgerows.

To make rose hip wine, chop or mince 1.75 kg/4 lb washed rose hips and place in a bucket with the finely pared rind and juice of 1 lemon and 1.5 kg/3 lb sugar. Pour on 4.5 l/8pts boiling water and stir. Dissolve 1 sachet wine yeast in a little warm water, leave for 5 minutes then stir it into the bucket. Stir daily for 12 days. Strain into a demijohn, top up with boiled water, seal with an airlock and leave in a warm place until fermentation stops. Siphon into a clean jar and leave to mature for 8 months before bottling.

Decorate a glass jar or enamel canister with pressed flowers then fill it with your home-made preserve to make an attractive gift. Glue individual pressed petals and leaves in a floral pattern on to the jar. Leave to dry thoroughly then cover with a few coats of varnish to protect the decoration.

Rose hip marmalade

Autumn is preserves time, but try something different from your usual blackberry jam. Simmer 1 kg/2 lb rose hips with 1.75 l/3pts water for about 45 minutes until tender, squashing occasionally. Pour into a jelly bag and drain overnight. Simmer 1 kg/2 lb prepared cooking apples until soft, add the rose hip juice and 750 g/1½ lb sugar and stir until the sugar has dissolved. Add 2 tbsp lemon juice and boil rapidly for about 10 minutes until setting point is reached. A spoonful of cooled jam will wrinkle when pressed. Pour into warm jars, seal and label.

Pick beech twigs just as the colour turns but before the leaves fall so that you can preserve them for dried arrangements.

Infuse 4 tbsp chopped mint overnight in 300 ml/½ pt full cream milk then strain and store in the refrigerator as a wonderful herbal moisturising milk.

September

The name lavender derives from the Latin word *lavare*, to wash, and it has long been associated with bathing and also with relaxation. Recipes in old herbal books have been discovered which recommend boiling a few handfuls of lavender flowers and a little salt in water to strain and add to bath water to refresh the body and clear the mind.

English lavender still produces the world's finest lavender water. The essential oils are, in fact, extracted from the bracts which enclose the flowers rather than the flowers themselves.

Lavender bottles

Old-fashioned lavender bottles used to be dried and used among stored clothes or linen to keep the fabric smelling sweet and free of moths. Cut long stalks of lavender on a dry day and gather into bunches of about 20 with the flower heads level. Tie the stalks together securely just under the heads. Bend the stalks back over to enclose the flowers.

Secure the stems and trim the ends.

22

Sage leaves used to be boiled in vinegar then applied as a hot poultice for sprains.

23

24

25

26

Lavender flower foam bath is easy to make. Dissolve 12 tbsp grated castile soap in 10 tbsp boiling water then stir in 4 tbsp crushed dried lavender flowers, stirring until the mixture is well blended. Pour into a bottle, cool, cover and label.

27

28

September

The glorious yellow flowers of *Oenothera erthrosepala* are just finishing their own season as the summer draws to a close, having flowered since early summer. The funnel-shaped blossoms have satiny petals which make excellent cut flowers.

Commonly known as the evening primrose, the flowers of some varieties open from a red-spotted bud towards the end of the day. The flowers last a few days before they fade.

Many herbal teas are associated with old-fashioned medicinal remedies. Basil was said to ease gastric troubles and catarrh. Borage was also believed to help with catarrh and was used as a tonic, as were dandelion, parsley and sage. Mint helped to relieve colds, headaches, sickness and heartburn and rosemary was good for headaches and insomnia.

Snapdragons

That childhood favourite the snapdragon, or antirrhinum, may still be flowering late in the season as it will continue to bear its fascinating blooms until the first frosts.

Scabious may also still be flowering now. If you leave some stems to run to seed, the attractive seed heads can be dried to use in winter arrangements.

29

Evening primrose oil is often taken as a food supplement to help maintain supple skin.

30

For a charming country-style herbal arrangement, pick several different types of herbs and make each type into a small bunch of a few stems each.

Arrange the herbs in a jug of water and finish off by placing a few marigolds or chrysanthemums amongst the green herbs.

October

'For you there's rosemary and rue, these keep
Seeming and savour all the winter long.'

William Shakespeare

October

maryllis belladonna was originally an African plant which can now be enjoyed in sheltered spots in temperate regions. It particularly likes the protection of a south-facing wall or fence in order to gain the maximum warmth from the summer sun.

The strap-shaped leaves appear in late winter and early spring followed by the sweetly scented flowers in September and October – a welcome flash of pink or white in the autumn garden.

If left undisturbed, new bulbs will develop and form clumps of plants over a period of years.

Pot-grown amaryllis

To bring colour into the house when fresh flowers become more expensive and less plentiful, you can buy amaryllis in pots to flower throughout the winter, or you can cultivate them yourself in a greenhouse.

The strong simplicity of gerbera daisies need a comparably bold touch when arranging. Try using a simple container such as this round glass goldfish bowl, and use plenty of flowers to give the arrangement body and shape

Some species of saxifrage are October-flowering, adding welcome colour to the rockery.

The time to prepare leaves for later dried arrangements is when they are at their peak. If you leave it too late, the leaves will drop.

October

Often confused with the geranium, it is more usually the pelargonium which we see in gardens, tubs, window boxes and hanging baskets, splashing the garden with blazes of bright reds, pinks and purples.

Because they are so free-flowering, they make ideal plants for cutting to enhance both formal and informal floral arrangements. When plant material is scarce at the end of the season, liven up a foliage display with a few carefully-placed blooms.

A country vase full of brilliant berries and rose hips echoes the tangled beauty of the autumn hedgerow. You can use any suitable materials such as crab apples, cotoneaster berries, rose hips and bright scarlet pelargonium

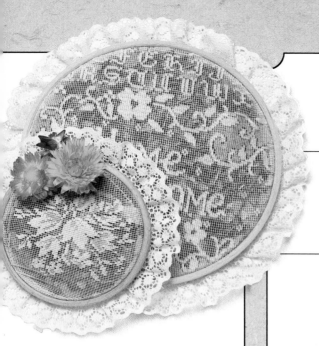

Herbal pillows

Hand-made gifts always have a special sentiment attached to them, and you can quite easily make prettily-shaped herbal sachets or pillows as gifts for family or friends. Decorate them with a little lace or an embroidered initial and fill with a soothingly-fragrant mixture of 4 tbsp each dried lavender flowers and dried rosemary leaves, 20 lightly crushed cloves and 1 tsp powdered dried orange rind.

8

9

10

11

12

13

From mid-summer to autumn, the beautiful crimson tassel-like flowers of Amaranthus caudatus, *or love lies bleeding, appear. If carefully dried, they retain their colour well.*

14

October

The chrysanthemum is a perennial favourite of flower-lovers, coming second only to the queen of flowers, the rose. In Britain, it first became fashionable at the end of the nineteenth century and has grown in popularity ever since. There are so many varieties offering different shapes, colours and patterns that it is impossible to become bored with this charming flower.

A simple jug of autumn flowers such as these chrysanthemums, hydrangea and Michaelmas daisies can be transformed into something unique by standing it with a harvest festival display of vegetables and fruits to create a dramatic still life. The rich, mellow colours of autumn are with us only briefly, but should be exploited while they are.

The golden flower of the East

First grown in China in 500 BC, the chrysanthemum epitomised the autumn for the ancient Chinese. The meaning they attributed to the plant is 'cheerfulness under adversity', perhaps because the flowers provide such a wonderful and long-lasting display just when the days are becoming shorter and colder.

15

*'Silence and sleep like fields
Of amaranth lie.'*

Walter de la Mare

16

17

18

19

20

21

*Giant poppy seed heads
develop a beautiful greyish
bloom and look wonderful
arranged informally in a
wicker basket. To save the
seeds for next year, hold the
heads downwards into a
paper bag and shake to
capture the precious seeds.*

October

Some people find the African violet, *Saintpaulia*, impossible to grow in the home – others cannot keep the smallest plant long before it bursts into flower. Certainly, in the right conditions – moist but never soggy, light and warm but not too sunny – it makes a wonderful house plant.

The heart-shaped leaves are dark green and velvety, contrasting with the profusion of purple or pink flowers with their distinctive yellow centres.

Even though the flowers are becoming fewer in the garden, there are always flowering pot plants which can decorate your home.

If you enjoy working with pressed flowers, investigate craft shops for kits such as presentation frames or trays. For best results, choose your colour scheme, make sure you have a range of materials and sketch out your design before you start. Then you can experiment by positioning leaves and petals in a pleasing arrangement before fixing them.

In the herb garden

It is a good time, now, to work in the herb garden, trimming back, tidying and generally preparing the plants for the winter.

For a winter supply of mint, that great favourite in the kitchen, pot up a few roots in a little compost and place them on a sunny kitchen window sill.

22

23

Now is a good time to start a flower diary, jotting down successes and failures in your garden to help your next year's planning.

24

25

26

27

Never waste your herbal cuttings. They can be dried ready for you to use in the kitchen.

28

October

The leaves and berries of the holly are a sure sign that we should be thinking about Christmas. They look wonderful in an evergreen arrangement of box and spruce surrounded by a rich collection of berries and nuts which will last for several weeks.

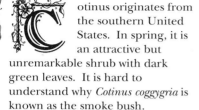

Cotinus originates from the southern United States. In spring, it is an attractive but unremarkable shrub with dark green leaves. It is hard to understand why *Cotinus coggygria* is known as the smoke bush.

In the summer, however, the reason becomes clear. The smoke bush seems to burst into life as the plant is smothered in a haze of wispy, pinkish, hairy flower stalks like a tangible mist.

In autumn, the leaves of all the varieties are transformed into a blaze of brilliant red, claret and orange, showing yet another face of this versatile and unusual plant.

29

'Most friendship is feigning, most loving mere folly.
Then heigh-ho! the holly! This life is most jolly.'

William Shakespeare

30

31

Bright autumn berries

Many plants which flower in spring
or summer produce the most
beautiful berries in the autumn. As
the colours of the season change
from the russets of autumn to the
reds and greens of winter, what
better way to create beauty inside
and out? Cotoneaster, berberis and
pyracantha are all wonderful shrubs
for autumn fruit displays.

November

'I never saw a moor,
I never saw the sea;
Yet know I how the heather looks,
And what a wave must be.'

Emily Dickinson

November

During the winter, many garden shrubs and plants produce flowers with beautiful scents. Gather everything you can find and group them together to enjoy them.

When you have flowers of widely differing character and size, they lose definition and importance if they are massed together in one vase and it is very difficult to make an attractive and harmonious arrangement.

However, if you collect together a group of small glasses – both stemmed, tall and squat to suit the individual flowers – you can create a balanced display which gives suitable emphasis to the individual blooms.

Black glass has a stark simplicity complemented by a striking colour contrast. The outline has been set with tall stems of ornamental chillies then filled in with a bold piece of ivy foliage at the back. Rose hips and chrysanthemums give the mass of colour, while the four strands of bear grass add elegance and movement with their stylish, curving graphic lines.

1

2

Where blew a flower may a flower no more
Lift its head to the blows of the rain.'
Dylan Thomas

3

4

5

Flowering pot plants in winter are nothing new.
Edwardian gardeners grew carnations, begonias and
poinsettias under glass to flower in November.

6

7

Bottle bank

Bottles can be used in the same way as glasses, collecting perhaps six or seven interesting ones and using them to display one or two flowers each.

Look out for old bottles at antique fairs or bric-a-brac stalls, as the thick, uneven glass and embossed lettering give extra character.

November

A child's straw hat makes a perfect base for a pretty wall decoration. Make a circle of wire to fit loosely over the crown of the hat. Wire short-stemmed flower heads to the circlet then pin or glue the finished ring over the hat. Add definition and a sense of fun with a bright ribbon to finish it off.

An arrangement of dried flowers can look just as stunning as fresh flowers, and in the winter when choice is limited and flowers are more expensive, can bring colour and life to your home. Baskets of all kinds provide excellent containers for dried flowers, beautifully complementing the lovely autumnal colours of many dried displays.

Scope and variety

Limit the different types of flowers you use for one arrangement otherwise it may begin to look cluttered; three or four different types are usually enough. You can often cleverly combine materials from your own garden with shop-bought flowers or a few evergreen sprigs. Be adventurous in your choice: try ears of wheat with silver honesty seed cases and ornamental peppers; or beech and molucella leaves with Chinese lanterns and dried amaranthus.

8

9

10

11

12

Little posies or arrangements of either fresh or dried flowers in a tiny vase look lovely on top of a special cake.

13

14

November

The hyacinths that grow in such profusion both in our gardens and our homes have all sprung from one hardy species, the tall and elegant *Hyacinthus orientalis*.

The striking flower spikes in yellows, blues, pinks and reds that are available in flower from nurseries from before Christmas until May are most commonly known as Dutch hyacinths. If you buy them in bud, you can keep them in a cool spot to prevent the flowers opening too quickly.

A mass of dried roses, delphiniums and gypsophilia give an opulent effect to this stunning decoration. Secure dry foam in the container so that it stands quite tall and in a dome shape then gradually cover the whole base with flowers.

Hyacinth jars

Hyacinths can be grown in water in tall vases with a constricted neck which are specially designed for the purpose.

Fill the jar almost to the neck with water and add a small lump of charcoal to keep the water fresh. Sit the hyacinth bulb in the top and keep the jar in a cool, dark place until the roots are about 10 cm/5 in long and leaves are showing, then move it to a warmer and lighter place.

Early Egyptians designed vases specially for specific flowers and often decorated them with flower motifs.

November

According to Chinese legend, the silk strands of silkworms were discovered in 2700 BC in a mulberry tree in the garden of the Emperor Huang-Ti. Whether or not this first silk was used to make flowers is doubtful, but certainly the Chinese were at the forefront of creating artificial flowers in paper, silk and precious metals.

With the advance of technology, high-quality silk flowers are now no longer as expensive as they once were and, while they can never replace fresh flowers, they do have a number of advantages. They do not wilt, require no special care and provide lasting beauty. Many are as near exact copies of specific flowers as possible, but you can also have fun with exotic silk flowers, fresh from the imagination of the designer.

Fabric flowers

Use the simple shapes of holly leaves, poinsettia or other favourite flowers to paint a design on napkins or place mats with brightly coloured fabric paints in festive colours of red, green and gold.

Porcelain and silver flowers with gilt stems were popular in the Edwardian era to create beautiful arrangements when fresh flowers were scarce.

Crêpe paper flowers make exciting place setting decorations. Crumple a piece of green paper over the top of a stub wire, stretch another piece of paper over the top and bind down to make the flower centre. Cut a 10 cm/4 in long strip of black paper 4 cm/1½ in wide and snip it at regular intervals. Twist each piece to make stamens and glue it around the flower centre. Gather about 6 petals around the centre and secure with thread or fine wire.

Arrange a few silk or dried flower heads over the top of a bowl of pot pourri for a pretty and fragrant table centre or decoration.

November

A picture of summer

Lovely pictures can be built up using pressed flowers and petals, carefully composed into patterns or representations of growing plants.

Use inspiration from any source when you are using plant material – whether fresh or dried. This charming selection of dried flowers echoes the rich colours and textures of an old tapestry. Hydrangeas, roses, sea lavender and poppy seed heads jostle together in a varied and exciting yet subtle arrangement.

To make the arrangement, wedge a block of foam into the basket so that it is level with the top. Position the larger flowers and sprays, such as the sea lavender, almost to cover the foam, then gradually fill in the gaps with the flower heads until the arrangement is brimming with flowers.

29

To curl florists' ribbon, simply pull down the ribbon
at a slight angle with the blade of a pair of scissors.

30

Wire a small flower head and twist the covered wire
around the stem of a wine glass.

A thick rope of plaited raffia hanging from the wall makes a stunning decoration when garnished with posies of dried flowers. Bind the ends of the rope securely and make a hanging loop at the top. Wire tiny bunches of helichrysum or other blooms then weave the wires into the rope and finish with curls of colourful ribbon.

December

'To me the meanest flower that blows can give
Thoughts that do often lie too deep for tears.'

William Wordsworth

December

A fruit bowl or a stemmed dish makes the perfect container for a spectacular table centre for a party or special occasion over the festive season.

When flowers are scarce, make use of glossy evergreen foliage and luscious fruit as the basis for your display, piling them into a dome. Short-stemmed roses and alstroemeria can be tucked in amongst the fruit and leaves. The flowers will easily last an evening or more to delight all your guests.

A little Christmas spray and a few pressed fern leaves can transform a pair of plain, dark-coloured gift boxes. Secure the leaves on the top of one box, spray with gold or silver and leave to dry. Lift the leaves and glue them to the top of the other box.

A Victorian kitchen

Old wooden kitchen equipment, such as wooden kitchen sieves, can be made into attractive little decorations with posies of dried flowers. To bring a touch of Victorian atmosphere to the kitchen, wire two wooden spoons together in a cross, decorate with a large satin bow and attach a few sprigs of dried grass and helichrysum flowers.

1

2

3

4

5

6

Cut paper flower garlands in the same way as you used to make paper dolls to decorate the edges of the tablecloth.

7

December

Flowering from December to February, the Christmas cactus, *Schlumbergera x buckleyi*, is aptly named. The large, curled magenta flowers make a wonderful display for the festive season.

The plants benefit from being outside during the summer months, from June to the middle of September, as this ripens the new growth. Find a spot sheltered from the bright sun but remember to bring the plants back indoors before the evenings become too cold.

Once the flower buds form, do not disturb the plant or let the soil dry out, otherwise the buds will drop and you will lose your Christmas display.

Endless sources

You should never think that there are no materials available for a floral arrangement – even in the dead of winter. Cast around for attractive foliage, dried rushes, seed cases or twigs and berries and you are sure to find enough for an attractive display. Mixing fresh and dried or silk materials can also make interesting combinations.

8

9

10

11

12

13

*'The mistletoe hung in the castle hall,
The holly branch shone on the old oak wall.'*

T.H. Bayly

14

The soft sheen of beech, molucella and fatsia leaves preserved in glycerine contrasts with the brilliant orange of Chinese lanterns and golden achillea. The bold shape of the design is established first by positioning the tall reeds before filling in the triangle and finishing with a splash of orange lanterns.

December

 nown to most people as the poinsettia, the true name of this plant is *Euphorbia pulcherrima,* probably the most popular house plant to use for Christmas decoration. It originated in Mexico, but can only be grown indoors in temperate regions.

The elliptic, bright green leaves are slightly lobed. The scarcely-significant little yellow flowers are surrounded by deep crimson bracts which make the plant so attractive.

Although the crimson form is the most common, scarlet, pink and white forms are also available.

Silver sprays

Spray some twigs silver and arrange them in a tall, simple vase. Suspend some brightly-coloured Christmas decorations from the twigs, keeping the lines clear and uncluttered, to give an elegant and stylish effect.

For a Christmas decoration in cool green and white, place a few scented freesias carefully with variegated ivies, euonymus, sprigs of yew and festive mistletoe. As a finishing touch, add a few gilded grapes.

15

16

17

18

19

In the 1920s and 1930s, the British Lady Astor had her gardeners produce poinsettias 2 m/6½ ft tall to decorate her home, Cliveden, at Christmas.

20

21

December

Cyclamen persicum originates from the eastern Mediterranean. The dark green leaves are marbled with silver, with the familiar petals borne on tall stems.

This is the progenitor of the winter-flowering pot plants which come in a variety of leaf shapes, petal colours and patterns to brighten our homes over Christmas and the New Year.

With a little care, the plants will continue to thrive in a warm room if kept quite moist by standing the pot on a saucer containing gravel and a little water. Otherwise they will suffer from the dry, overhot atmosphere of centrally-heated rooms.

Christmas colours

It creates a very stylish effect if you limit the colour schemes of your decorations. Green, red and white offer an attractive and traditional combination, or if you prefer, choose something entirely different and pair silver with pinks for a delicate and feminine effect.

A garland made on
a foam base can be used
flat as a table decoration or hung on a door
or wall. Fir forms the basis of the garland,
interleaved with a few sprigs of silver
variegated euonymus and studded with
berries, rose hips and scarlet anemones.

22

23

24

25

What prettier way to finish a gift than to top it with
a few precious fresh flowers?

December

C ombine the festive feel of candlelight with your flowers at Christmas time.

A basket brimming with Christmas foliage can be brought alive with a few tall red candles, red roses and tiny presents wrapped in a glossy paper to reflect the light. Sprigs of gypsophilia look like frosted snowflakes among the winter greenery.

Cut shapes of poinsettia bracts and leaves from shiny card and fix them round a cane ring for an unusual Christmas wreath. You can buy yellow stamens from craft shops to finish the centres. Paper flowers (Nov 22) can be wired on to a foam or polystyrene ring in a mass of glorious colour.

Flowers and light

Flowers lit in different ways can take on quite different appearances. Most arrangements look their best with a gentle, all-over lighting with a stronger side light to bring out form and colour. In a room with no natural light, choose shapes which are bold and sculptural and silhouette against a pale, plain background. Stand pale flowers against a dark background to throw them into relief.

The ancient Romans loved flowers and often wove flower garlands and headdresses to enliven their celebrations.

Index

**Dates refer to the first day of
the spread**